TURKANA

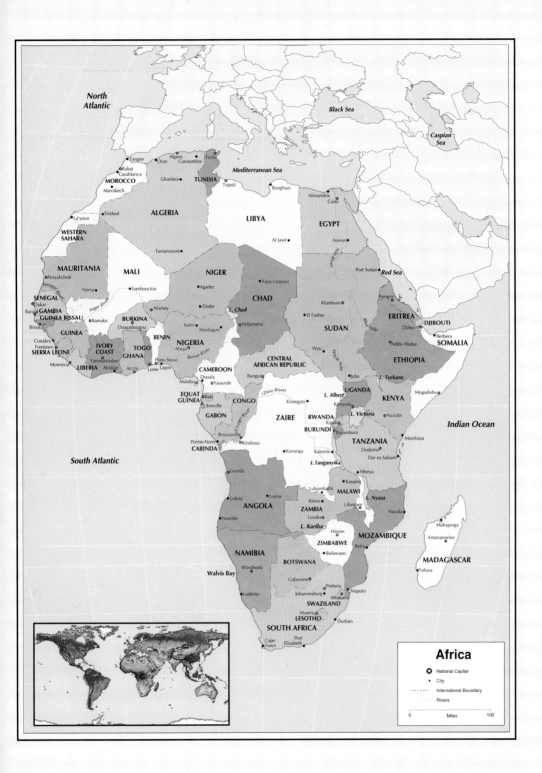

North
Atlantic

Black Sea

Caspian
Sea

Tangier
Algiers
Oran
Constantine
Tunis

MOROCCO
Rabat
Casablanca

Ghardaia
TUNISIA

Marrakech

Mediterranean Sea

Tripoli

Banghazi

Alexandria
Cairo

La'youn
Tindouf

WESTERN
SAHARA

ALGERIA

LIBYA

EGYPT

Aswan

Al Jawf

Tamanrasset

Port Sudan
Red Sea

MAURITANIA
Nouakchott

MALI

NIGER

Faya-Largeau

Asmera
ERITREA
DJIBOUTI

Nema

Tombouctou

Agadez

Khartoum

Djibouti
Berbera

SENEGAL
Dakar
Banjul
GAMBIA
GUINEA BISSAU
Bissau

Niamey
Zinder

CHAD

L. Chad

SUDAN

Blue Nile

Addis Ababa
SOMALIA

Bamako
BURKINA
Ouagadougou

Kano

Ndjamena

El Fasher

ETHIOPIA

GUINEA
Conakry
Freetown
SIERRA LEONE
Monrovia
LIBERIA

BENIN
IVORY
COAST
TOGO
Yamoussoukro
GHANA
Abidjan
Accra

Maidugun

Abuja
NIGERIA
Porto Novo
Lome
Lagos

Benue River

CAMEROON
Douala

Wau

CENTRAL
AFRICAN REPUBLIC

White Nile

Juba

L. Turkana

EQUAT
GUINEA
Malabo
Bata
Libreville

Yaounde

Bangui

(Zaire River)

UGANDA

L. Albert

Kisangani

Kampala
L. Victoria

KENYA

Mogadishu

Indian Ocean

CONGO

GABON

ZAIRE

RWANDA
Kigali
BURUNDI
Bujumbura

Nairobi

South Atlantic

Brazzaville
Pointe-Noire
CABINDA
Kinshasa

Congo River

Kanaga

Kalemie

TANZANIA
Dodoma
Dar es Salaam

Mombasa

L.Tanganyika

Luanda

Mbeya

Kasama

Lobito
Luena

Lubumbashi
MALAWI

L. Nyasa

ANGOLA
Kitwe
ZAMBIA

Lilongwe

Nacala

Namibe

Lusaka

L. Kariba

Harare

MOZAMBIQUE

Mahajanga

ZIMBABWE
Bulawayo

Beira

Antananarivo

NAMIBIA

BOTSWANA

MADAGASCAR
Toliara

Walvis Bay
Windhoek

Gaborone
Pretoria
Maputo
Johannesburg
Mbabane

Luderitz
SWAZILAND
Maseru
LESOTHO
Durban
SOUTH AFRICA
Cape
Town
Port
Elizabeth

Africa

⊛ National Capital

• City

---- International Boundary

~~~ Rivers

0   Miles   100

The Heritage Library of African Peoples

TURKANA

Chieka Ifemesia, Ph.D.

THE ROSEN PUBLISHING GROUP, INC.
NEW YORK

Published in 1996 by The Rosen Publishing Group, Inc.
29 East 21st Street, New York, New York 10010

First Edition

Manufactured in the United States of America.

Library of Congress Cataloging-in-Publication Data

Ifemesia, Chieka.
    Turkana / Chieka Ifemesia. — 1st ed.
      p. cm. — (The Heritage library of African peoples)
    Includes bibliographical references and index.
    ISBN 0-8239-1761-4
    1. Turkana (African people)—Juvenile literature. [1. Turkana
(African people)] I. Title. II. Series.
DT433.545.T87I35   1995
960′.04965—dc20   95-13691
                                        CIP
                                        AC

Contents

INTRODUCTION

THERE IS EVERY REASON FOR US TO KNOW
something about Africa and to understand its
past and the way of life of its peoples. Africa is a
rich continent that has for centuries provided
the world with art, culture, labor, wealth, and
natural resources. It has vast mineral deposits,
fossil fuels, and commercial crops.

But perhaps most important is the fact that
fossil evidence indicates that human beings
originated in Africa. The earliest traces of
human beings and their tools are almost two
million years old. Their descendants have
migrated throughout the world. To be human is
to be of African descent.

The experiences of the peoples who stayed in
Africa are as rich and as diverse as of those who
established themselves elsewhere. This series of
books describes their environment, their modes
of subsistence, their relationships, and their customs and beliefs. The books present the variety
of languages, histories, cultures, and religions
that are to be found on the African continent.
They demonstrate the historical linkages between
African peoples and the way contemporary Africa
has been affected by European colonial rule.

Africa is large, complex, and diverse. It en-
compasses an area of more than 11,700,000

square miles. The United States, Europe, and India could fit easily into it. The sheer size is an indication of the continent's great variety in geography, terrain, climate, flora, fauna, peoples, languages, and cultures.

Much of contemporary Africa has been shaped by European colonial rule, industrialization, urbanization, and the demands of a world economic system. For more than seventy years, large regions of Africa were ruled by Great Britain, France, Belgium, Portugal, and Spain. African peoples from various ethnic, linguistic, and cultural backgrounds were brought together to form colonial states.

For decades Africans struggled to gain their independence. It was not until after World War II that the colonial territories become independent African states. Today, almost all of Africa is ruled by Africans. Large numbers of Africans live in modern cities. Rural Africa is also being transformed, and yet its people still engage in many of their customs and beliefs.

Contemporary circumstances and natural events have not always been kind to ordinary Africans. Today, however, new popular social movements and technological innovations pose great promise for future development.

George C. Bond, Ph.D., Director
Institute of African Studies
Columbia University, New York

The Turkana live in northwest Kenya, in East Africa.

1

THE LAND OF THE TURKANA

MOST OF THE PEOPLE KNOWN AS THE TURKANA live in northwestern Kenya, in East Africa. Numbering well over 200,000, they occupy an irregular rectangular area bordered by Lake Turkana and Ethiopia on the east, northeastern Uganda on the west, and southern Sudan on the north. Some Turkana also live in Sudan. The neighbors of the Turkana to the southwest are the Pokot people. To the southeast are the Samburu, into whose upland districts some Turkana have moved.

Turkanaland lies on the floor of the Great Rift Valley, which cuts across a good part of Kenya and Tanzania. The territory of the Turkana occupies an area of about 23,500 square miles and is on the average about 2,000 feet lower than the surrounding country.

In many parts of the land, rock and lava are

SUDAN

ETHIOPIA

• Addis Ababa

• Juba

Lake Turkana

Lokitaung

Tarach R.

Lodwar

Turkwell R.

Lokichar

TURKANA

Kerio R.

Lake Albert

UGANDA

• Buna

Marsabit

Milgis River

Wajir

SOMALIA

• Kitale

RIFT VALLEY

Eldoret •

Uaso Nyiro River

Kampala
•

Kisumu
•

KENYA

Liboi

Kericho

•Garissa

Lake Victoria

• Embu

Thika •

Nairobi

Lamu •

TANZANIA

Malindi

Galana River

Voi •

Indian
Ocean

Mombasa •

AFRICA (KENYA)

TURKANA

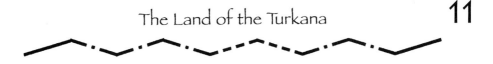

widespread and the rainfall is low, about 15 to 25 inches per year. The country has just enough vegetation—mostly brushwood and scrub—for sheep, goats, and camels to graze. Cattle require lusher grasses, and so are found chiefly on the banks of rivers and mountainsides. The upper basin of the largest river, the Turkwell, and other watercourses such as the Kerio have thick tropical vegetation. Similarly, grass is taller and trees are thicker on the largest mountains, whose peaks are actually covered with forest.

The Turkana are mainly a pastoral people. They have adapted to soil and water shortages by learning to rear camels instead of cows. Camels are found even in central Turkanaland and the area immediately to the west of Lake Turkana, where they survive the most arid desert.▲

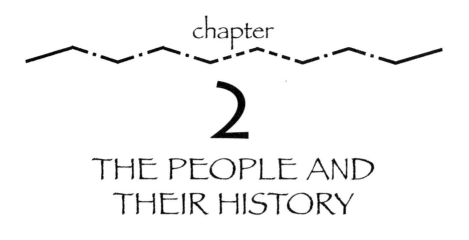

chapter

2

THE PEOPLE AND
THEIR HISTORY

THE TURKANA BELONG TO THE COLLECTION OF ethnic groups usually known as the Eastern Nilotes. They are called Nilotes because their ancient homeland was near the headwaters of the Nile River.

The Turkana are the largest of the seven ethnic groups that make up what is called the Karamajong Cluster; others are the Karamajong, Jie, Dodos, Toposa, Donyiro, and Jiye. Members of the Karamajong Cluster all speak dialects of Teso. The Turkana speak a specific dialect, called Turkana after the people themselves. Each of the peoples of the Karamajong Cluster live in the vicinity of Turkanaland.

Oral traditions of the Karamajong people tell of relatively recent activities around Turkanaland. They describe how, about 400 to 500 years ago, the Karamajong migrated from Apuli, a place in the

This young woman is wearing a style of beadwork and hairdressing traditional to the Turkana.

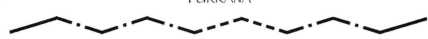

northeast of their present land. The tradition adds that not long afterward a group of youth from the Jieland section of Karamajong, looking for a stray ox, found themselves in the valley of the Tarash River. There they met an old Turkana woman who was gathering wild fruit. The travelers were much impressed by the relatively rich, unoccupied land and the abundance of berries in the place. On their return to Jieland, the young men were joined by other young men and women in a migration with their livestock down the escarpment into what is known today as Turkanaland.

This story represents the love for wandering that has long characterized the Turkana. Such movement was especially likely when population increase brought about crowding. The migrations probably took place in successive sweeps. It is also likely that other people of similar origin—or of different origins but who quickly assimilated—joined the earlier immigrants. Over time, the population of Turkana-speaking people grew to many times what it was in Jieland.

From two centers in the valleys of the Turkwell and the Kagwalasi (or Nakwehe), both rivers that feed into Lake Turkana, the Turkana later spread eastward to the western shores of the lake. There they dislodged the Samburu, the former inhabitants. The Turkana also extended into the more fertile lands of their kinsmen—the

Dodos, Karamajong, Toposa, and Donyiro—as well as into the territories of the Pokot to the southwest and of the Marile on the northwestern shore of the lake.

The Turkana oral tradition recalls nothing else about their past except for periodic visits of Swahili traders. However, when the first European travelers visited the Turkana of the lake region in 1888, they found that the people were not only firmly settled in their present territory but had built a formidable fighting force.▲

3

SOCIAL AND POLITICAL ORGANIZATION

THE NUCLEAR FAMILY IS THE BASIC SOCIAL AND political unit among the Turkana. The family comprises a man, his wife or wives, his sons and their wives and children, and his unmarried daughters. In the homestead there might also be a grandparent or other relative and a concubine (a woman living in a the household to whom he is not married.)

The man is the head of the family. The family is represented economically by its herd of livestock. However, the family herd is divided among the wives, mostly to ensure that the children have enough milk to drink. As they grow, each child has his or her own animals. The remaining cattle in the herd are normally held by the senior wife of the head, but they all belong to him. This residual herd is used on behalf of the family for general meat supplies and for gifts,

The nuclear family is the basic social and political unit among the Turkana.

payments, and other social and economic commitments.

The Turkana homestead (*awi*) is never meant to be a permanent establishment. It is built with thorn boughs, brushwood, and palm leaves. Still, while it exists, the homestead physically makes an important social and political statement. In the outer circular fence around the homestead, the main entrance (*ekidor*) always faces the east. A short way behind this entrance are the sleeping quarters and fireplace (*etiem*) of the homestead head; this allows him to benefit each morning from the enlivening influence

The Turkana homestead is not meant to be a permanent structure.

of the rising sun. To the right of the entrance, inside the enclosure, are the day and night huts (*ngkalia*) of the senior wife, and to the left those of the other wives in order of seniority. Next to the left around the enclosure are the dwellings of the widowed mother and the concubine of the homestead head. At the center of the homestead are an open yard and enclosures for livestock. The homesteads of richer men are built with more comfortable shelters.

Not all the members of a man's family may live in one homestead throughout the year. It is largely the needs of the livestock that decide where members of the family are. Usually dur-

The Turkana move frequently. Their moves are sometimes dictated by changing seasons, other times by the needs of the individual family members.

ing the rainy season, the cattle are at the chief homestead (*awi napolon*), where the man, the senior wife, her young children, and other dependents live and care for the small livestock. But at the peak of the dry season other members of the family may be distributed between two or more homesteads. These other homesteads may be cattle camps (*awi abor*) set up to stretch out the large herds of a rich family over a wider area. The homesteads may also separate the cattle and sheep from the camels and goats.

People also move from one homestead to

Donkeys are usually used to transport belongings from the site of one homestead to another.

another for personal reasons. A sick wife or a nursing mother may switch homesteads with another woman, to be nearer a source of milk or healing specialists. Whatever arrangement is made, everyone makes a point of regularly returning to base, to the chief homestead, where all rituals pertaining to the family are performed.

▼ THE EXTENDED FAMILY ▼

Among the Turkana, the extended family (*ngitungakothi*) is made up of all males who can claim common descent on the male side. The unit

could go back three or four generations. To members of the group, those within it are "our people." But strictly speaking, the extended family also includes the wives of each of these men if they have raised a child to walking stage. It excludes women who have married elsewhere and are no longer in the family.

The core of the extended family, however, is essentially the son of a deceased father, his full brothers, his half-brothers, and his paternal male first cousins, along with the nuclear families of all these men. The members of an extended family interact during various rituals, which establish the role of each person within the group. The head of the extended family is highlighted at the second funeral ceremony of an important member. The occasion is attended by all members with their cattle, primarily to celebrate the common origins of their herds. There, by the ritual enacted by the head, the senior man exercises leadership over the extended family. Members also share fellowship on other such occasions as initiation, weddings, and judicial compensation, when there is mutual assistance in giving and receiving livestock.

▼ THE CLAN ▼

Every Turkana belongs to a clan (*ateger*), of which there are about 20. They fall into two major types: the large, widespread clans, each

Turkanaland has large areas of vast, open land with relatively little rainfall.

comprising over 1,000 adult males, and the very small ones consisting of only about 30 members.

Clans are of little practical or political importance to the Turkana today, especially since clans no longer own herds or pastures or watering places, all of which usually bring and keep the people together. Nor do traveling Turkana any longer expect help or hospitality from fellow clansmen. They would expect that help from bond-friends, people in various parts of the country to whom they have made a ritual commitment.

Clans meant a great deal more in the past. All cattle are still branded with the clan marks. The people also maintain that, both in blood and in spirit, "all clansmen are brothers." Because a clan is another kind of family, it is forbidden to marry within one's own clan. The observance of clan ritual is entrusted to the women. Clan rules are secret. Women also guard the regulations

concerning dress and proper behavior during
pregnancy.

▼ THE NEIGHBORHOOD ▼

The Turkana word for neighborhood (*adakar*)
generally refers to people who graze their livestock in a particular area, be it in the foothills,
on a river bank, or in wide plains. Socially, the
word means all those who can freely assemble
for a feast or a dance.

The neighborhood is the Turkana community
that cuts across family, homestead, and clan
lines. A Turkana neighborhood is a series of
units that grow progressively larger and include
more people. The smallest units contain one to
five homesteads, no two being more than two
minutes' walk apart. And although the families
are basically autonomous, they sometimes share
food. Within this neighborhood, the men meet
to talk under a shady tree or band together for a
trading journey. The women visit with each
other or work their gardens in adjoining plots.
The herdboys play together in the pastures be-
side their livestock. The girls take cattle to a
common watering place. The eligible young men
and women get to know one another.

A larger unit of neighborhood system includes
homesteads spread over an area up to five
square miles. The heads of these connected
homesteads join together to organize community

projects. They might plan the sharing of a large watering place; the slaughtering by a homestead—in rotation every six to ten days throughout the year—of an animal for a meat feast; the offering of communal prayers at religious ceremonies, as the need arises; and the staging of different types of dances.

A third neighborhood entity is very vague. It can cover an area whose radius one can normally walk in one day. The many homesteads in this locality do not generally act as a unit but may be present at the same weddings, dances, and other major ceremonies, and the whole vicinity may be served by the same religious leaders.

▼ THE TERRITORIAL ORGANIZATION ▼

The largest unit of social organization among the Turkana is the territory. The territory is not as important now as it was in earlier times when the Turkana lived together and interacted more closely for initiations and other events. Today, however, two unequal territorial divisions comprise the People of the Plains (Ngicuro) and the People of the Forest (Ngimonia). Each division is made up of sections. The Ngicuro occupy five sections in the west, and the Ngimonia fourteen sections in the north and east. Traditionally the people of the Plains and the Forest differed in details of women's dress and adornments, and of

Turkana women may carry as much as eight to ten gallons of water from a
watering hole and walk for three to five miles back to the homestead.

This older Turkana woman is wearing a copper wire lip plug fitted through a hole pierced in her lower lip, a traditional piece of Turkana jewelry.

the ritual performed at the sacrifice of an ox.

Among the Forest People in the wetter upper basin of the Turkwell River live the Ngabotok, a group of a rather different character from other Turkana. For over two hundred years the Ngabotok have been settled farmers and honey-gatherers whom other Turkana have regarded as stockless and poor. But they now have the great advantage of being both cultivators and livestock keepers. Territorial divisions do not really affect Turkana plans and movements. With their live-stock they roam freely over all parts of their land.

Nevertheless, because families and clans tend to identify with certain places, the Turkana are aware of the resentment attached to roaming into someone else's familiar haunt. This resent-ment can develop into hostility.

▼ JUSTICE ▼

The punishment of crime and the settlement of disputes are communal affairs among the Turkana. Traditions of law depend on a people's moral principles and the values that they hold in common. Among the Turkana parents teach their young children the taboos of the commu-nity: never to be cowardly, never to lie, steal, slander, bear false witness, be unkind to chil-dren, neglect old people, and so forth. Fights between extended families are looked upon as serious issues, and neighbors will hasten to stop such disharmony because it disrupts the community. Order and peace in the community are the responsibility of all.

When a dispute occurs, the offended party initiates action. Observers take an active part in bringing about a settlement. Each side is supported by a group that usually includes members of the nuclear family and homestead, a man's mother and wife's (or wives') kin, and bond-friends. All of these people have an interest in the man's payment or receipt of compensation.

Turkana society is made up of small communities in which everybody claims to know everybody else's character, and people believe they can readily trace the course of events. Collectively, there is little difficulty in determining who is guilty or innocent in a quarrel. Compensations are decided according to the seriousness of the offense. Traditionally, the most serious offenses were homicide and adultery.

Often some form of revenge would be taken by the victim of just such a serious crime. Grief and anger in the offended man's family could immediately lead to the death of the offender or of a member of his family. Otherwise, as many head of livestock as possible would be seized from the suspect's animals and those of his family until the matter was settled. A reconciliation took place at a special public ceremony, where

This young girl shows scars on her stomach, the result of a shaman's treatment.

A Turkana warrior.

the injured family finally declared themselves satisfied, and both parties announced the end of the dispute. Where there had been friendly relations and it was accidental homicide, however, the issue might be resolved in such an amicable manner as giving a daughter in marriage. Only the killing of a publicly acknowledged witch was never compensated.

Other lesser offenses such as physical injuries and impregnating an unmarried girl are settled by a payment of livestock. The number and composition of animals vary according to the severity of the injury, the resources of the offender and his family, and how keenly the act is felt by the offended. Other disagreements may be resolved by a fight with sticks if feelings get out of control, but no compensation is normally paid. A person who insists that he or she is not guilty may take a solemn oath of innocence by stepping over crossed spears. The Turkana believe that if any guilty man did this, Akuj (the High God) would take his life or that of a member of his family or of his livestock.▲

4

ECONOMIC PURSUITS

THE MAJORITY OF TURKANA RAISE LIVESTOCK. The nature of their country has determined the types of animals they keep and the role these animals play in their economy.

Cattle are central to the economic life of the Turkana. Cattle graze during the short wet season, feeding on the tall grass in some areas and on scrub grass that survives in drier places. Men and boys lead the cattle to pasture and water. Even when the best pasture is near the homestead, the watering place may be as far as a whole night's walk away. As a result, cattle may graze only every other day. The same thing happens when the camp is near the water and the cattle have to travel a long distance for good pasture.

Women and girls milk the cattle, usually twice a day: at sunrise and sunset. Four to five pints

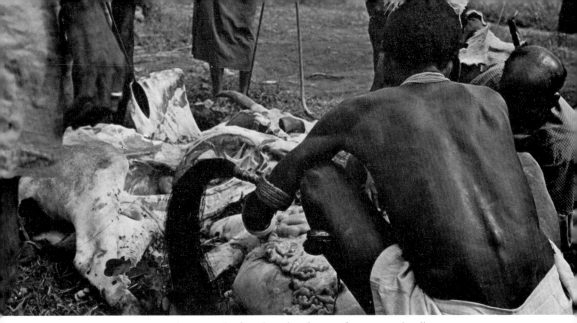

Cattle provide food in the form of meat and milk.

of milk can be collected from a cow in the wet season, and about one pint in the dry season. During an abundant period, large quantities of milk are boiled and made into dried milk (*edodo*), which is kept for use during the lean season. Cattle provide food not only in the form of milk but also as blood (especially on ritual and ceremonial occasions) and meat, on both of which the Turkana family heavily relies. Butter and ghee (semiliquid butter purified by boiling) are also made. Cattle droppings are used as fuel, and their urine as soap for washing.

The acquisition of camels is one of the positive developments that have influenced the Turkana since their arrival in their present region. In the early to mid-1950s, Turkana men could recall the times times when they raided the Rendille and Booran for camels. Camels can thrive in the grassless semidesert scrubland that comprises most of

33

Camels are the ideal animal for the environment and lifestyle of the Turkana.

Turkanaland, and they can go without water for three or more days. Thus, for doing even less work than herding cattle, the Turkana get much more from camels. Camels are milked four to seven times a day. More blood and meat are available from a camel than from a cow or bull.

Although for these reasons camels are rated equally with cattle for economic transactions such as negotiating compensation or bride-wealth, in social affairs generally camels are not so highly regarded. People do not keep personal camels, for instance, whereas they sometimes have a cow that is special to them; and some men may have no camels at all but a large herd

of cattle. There are no songs or dances about camels as there are about cattle. Nor are camels used for transportation, even when the homestead moves.

The Turkana also rear sheep and goats. Sheep prefer to eat tall grasses, but they can survive browsing on brush. Goats feed on the same pasture as camels and can be herded by small boys and girls around the homestead. But while cattle can be left to themselves, sheep, goats, and camels tend to stray, so they have to be closely watched. At sundown, search parties hasten to find and bring home missing animals. Very young animals are kept within the homestead enclosure and food is brought to them.

The special beast of burden for the Turkana is the donkey. One woman alone may own as many as five. All donkeys from neighboring homesteads are collected into a large herd to graze together. The Turkana neither drink donkey milk nor eat its meat. But strips of the hide are used for making saddle packs, to carry household goods and very young animals when a homestead is moving. A donkey's burden may also include very old or sick persons in the family. And yet, socially, donkeys are mocked and despised by the Turkana.

The migrations of the Turkana are directed by the needs of the livestock. Their nomadic life involves not only the daily search for pasture and water, but also seasonal movement, known as transhumance. Both the daily and seasonal migrations continue year-round. Because the vegetation in Turkana country varies so greatly, the people are also forced to make separate arrangements for their cattle and for other animals. In the dry season (*akumo*), cattle, sometimes accompanied by sheep, move from the arid plains to the foothills and mountainsides to the north and west, whereas the camels and goats move near the banks of the principal rivers in central and southern Turkanaland. During the short wet season (*agiboro*) there is sufficient pasture in the plains and riverbanks for all the animals and their herders to stay together as much as possible around the chief homestead.

▼ SOIL CULTIVATION ▼

The Turkana have traditionally engaged in the cultivation of the soil, but not to any great extent. Wherever the homestead may happen to be, a wife chooses a depression in the surrounding land or a spot near a river or stream known to flood over the adjoining land in the wet season. The periodic flooding brings moisture and nutrients to the soil. She plants millet and gourds. The women return annually during the rains to cultivate these family gardens. After about three to five years the land is allowed to lie fallow.

The grain reaped in any one year can hardly be enough for family needs. Especially in the dry season, the people make do with grain from other Turkana areas, like the lands of the Ngabotok and the deltas of the Turkwell and Kerio rivers. Nowadays grain has also been obtained from stores in Turkanaland and from grain-growers in Ethiopia and Uganda. Numerous varieties of berries and nuts abound. The Turkana turn them into something like cornmeal by pounding and drying. They then form the meal into cakes by crushing it and mixing it with milk. In this way they can preserve the meal for a long time.

▼ FISHING ▼

There have always been some Turkana who, despite Turkana tradition, have no livestock and instead are fishermen. They live on the western shore of Lake Turkana. During the dry season they are joined in fishing by some stockowners whose pastures are near the lake. The fish caught are roasted and boiled for eating. Today fishing is seen by many Turkana as a viable way to make a living.

▼ ARTS AND CRAFTS ▼

In spite of their mobile lifestyle, the Turkana produce many beautiful arts and crafts. Their handiwork can be found in curio shops in the cities of Kenya. The Turkana work skillfully with

This Turkana elder sits on a stool made of wood.

almost every material in their environment and beyond. They produce various household vessels: decorated wooden water containers; pots made from camel hide for holding milk, butter, fat, and other foods; leather bottles and drinking vessels. To these have been added digging sticks and fish traps.

The Turkana make stools of wood. Hides are

A senior Turkana rests on his headstool, designed to help preserve his traditional hairstyle.

used for sleeping and for keeping out the rain, and as soles for sandals. Sheep and goat skins are used for women's clothing. Animal horns serve as containers for feathers and tobacco. Turkana weapons include spears and shields (of giraffe, buffalo, or hippopotamus hide), wrist-knives, and fighting sticks.

The Turkana adorn themselves elaborately with numerous articles of clothing and ornate headdresses, using hide and leather, beads, feathers, seeds, nuts, ostrich eggshells, metal, and other materials.▲

chapter

5

OTHER ASPECTS
OF CULTURE

AN IMPORTANT FEATURE IN THE CULTURAL LIFE of the Turkana is age-grouping and initiation. At birth, every male Turkana belongs to one of two groups: Stones (*ngimur*) or Leopards (*ngerisai*). When a male child is born in wedlock, he takes the group opposite to that of his father. For example, if the father is a Stone, the son at once becomes a Leopard. But if the son is born outside wedlock, he takes the group opposite his mother's father; sometimes this may be the same group as that of his real father.

Stones and Leopards are grouped under different shade trees during the initiation ceremony. Decorations and body ornaments distinguish members of the two groups in adulthood. Even today a man's wife might wear a neck ring that is silver in color if her husband is a Stone or a brass ring if he is a Leopard. The groups

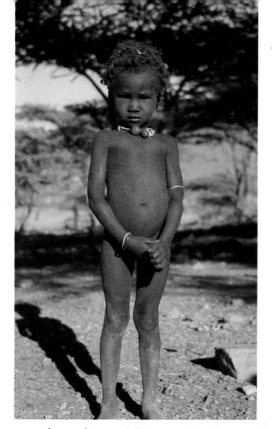

Among the Turkana, children are highly regarded.

are also recognized at all important ceremonies, where a sheep is slaughtered for each band.

A boy's group is of little importance to him, however, until he has been initiated according to custom. Initiation takes place when youths are between the ages of 16 and 20. It is held in a good wet season when there is enough food for such a large community celebration. There should also be at least six candidates. Sometimes boys have to wait several years to be initiated until enough youths have come of age to make the celebration worth staging.

All boys initiated at once belong to the same age-set or group (*athapan*). A boy's position is

determined by his father's position in the age-set system. But if all initiates' fathers belong to the same age-set, then each father's position within the age-set determines his son's position among his fellow initiates and in the rest of the Turkana community. Thus even the youngest son of an old man may be given the most senior position among his fellow initiates.

The Turkana initiation candidates must perform a task demanding personal strength, skill, and accuracy: the precise spearing of an animal to death. The initiate's father provides a male animal—an ox for the first son, a male goat for the second, an ox again for the third, and so on for the rest. After the candidates of each group have been placed in the proper seniority order, each comes in turn to spear his animal to death in one throw. The elders cut open each animal's stomach and smear the initiate's body with its contents. The elders bless the initiates, telling them that they are now men. Great feasting, rejoicing, and merrymaking by the whole community then follow.

Each initiate then proceeds to the house of his patron. This is an older man of the initiate's group chosen by his family and living at a distance. There the initiate hands over to his patron whatever possessions he has (spear, stool, cloth, beds, sandals, etc.) and goes into seclusion for about five days. During his stay, the youth car-

Once his initiation is complete, a young man takes his place in Turkana society by participating in ceremonies and festivals, and by marrying.

ries out chores at his patron's homestead and demonstrates in every way that he is now a responsible adult. Before the novice's return home, the patron presents him with new possessions befitting a Turkana man. For the rest of their lives an intimate relationship exists between the two men.

A Turkana girl does not belong to any particular group until she marries, when she joins her husband's group.

On completing the entire process of initiation, the young man can now, in the eyes of the people, take part on his own in the periodic ceremonies and festivals and engage in courtship leading to marriage. His friend and former patron gives him an ox at his marriage.

The initiation for girls is even more closely connected with marriage. The ceremony is conducted in the wet season shortly before or after the wedding, before the wife becomes a mother. A girl does not belong to any group at birth or at initiation, but rather at marriage, when she joins her husband's group.

At the girls' initiation, the senior wives of the

more senior men in the neighborhood, who are the sponsors of the ceremony, do not arrange the candidates in any order of seniority. Instead, the candidates are brought together in an open community ground and ordered to do homestead and household jobs to test their skills. From there the participants and their husbands walk into a nearby bush. The men kill the oxen and smaller animals that the women's fathers and husbands have provided for the occasion. Everyone feasts, then stays overnight in the bush. The initiates are given a group name as they return home the next morning.

▼ BOND-FRIENDSHIP ▼

Just as Turkana men form friendships with age-mates in the neighborhood with whom they share their initiation, they also form bond-friendships (*talupainon*) with men from distant parts of Turkana country and beyond. Two such friends may not live in the same area, but rather some thirty or forty miles apart, and may have met during their trading and other journeys.

Bond-friendships are often confirmed by a form of livestock deal, a practice that brings mutual benefit to both parties. The giving of cattle is a kind of insurance in times of plenty that will minimize or offset some unexpected losses in times of disaster. The giver of livestock is respected in the community for his generosity.

At the same time, the receiver may now have part of the resources he needs for bridewealth or some other special ceremony; or for enlarging his herd, obtaining more dairy products, and improving his own social position. Bond-friends come to the help of bond-friends also by sharing their pastureland during a drought season.

▼ MARRIAGE ▼

The sphere of life in which the independent Turkana has the greatest need for the support of others is marriage. To the Turkana, marriage is in many ways a family affair. Although a young man looks for a woman he likes, his parents must approve. His father ensures that the livestock for bridewealth is available and gives his permission and blessing. His mother must be satisfied that the girl is a good and hard worker in order to give her approval. The whole family has to be satisfied that no blood relationship can be traced between the young man and woman on either side of the family, and that the woman's family can afford the traditional gift exchange of livestock between the two families.

Sometimes two young people elope, especially if the bride's parents are resisting the proposal, or just for fun and excitement. In any case, the adventure is followed by discussion between the families. No matter how the marriage takes place, there must always be a bridewealth.

Children are expected soon after marriage.

The young man opens the discussion by visiting with a few age-mates the bride's father with a gift of tobacco and one or two goats. The suitor makes his interest known and, in a joking talk with the woman's father, also gets to know whether he approves and further talks can proceed.

Negotiations for bridewealth are carried on between the two families. There is no standing number or composition of livestock. A man gives what he has. That usually consists of cattle, camels, sheep, and goats. Donkeys are included if requested. The suitor produces about half the expected number of animals from his own herd, and the rest come from the family, bond-friends, and other connections.

On the day of the marriage ceremony (*akotar*) the groom, dressed in leopard skin and ostrich feathers, is accompanied by his extended family, all festively dressed, to the homestead of the bride. There he kills the marriage ox (*emon akotar*) within the homestead enclosure. The bond is sealed as the male relatives of the bride and groom's families drink the ox blood and participate in the meat feast prepared by the women of the bride's family. All the men present hold a dance, while the women of the groom's family dance from hut to hut in the homestead, and finally take the bride away to their own homestead. The next morning, the groom's mother and fellow wives distribute the bride's

girlhood dresses and decorations among the girls of the family and replace them with clothing proper for a wife. They put a little child on her lap to signify what is expected before long.

Marriage is when a man advances in family seniority. Following his marriage, a man sets up his own homestead apart from his father's. He also begins to raise his own herd, using the animals from his mother's herd as the core. Yet he continues to tend his father's herd. When his children are old enough to become his own herdboys, the man can establish an autonomous homestead of his own by adding to his herd gifts from his father and his wife's family. Nevertheless, by law and custom, the man cannot use this herd of livestock without the permission of his father. A man is not considered independent until his father has died.

▼ RELIGION ▼

The Turkana believe in one great High God (Akuj), who lives in the sky above the clouds. The Turkana believe that Akuj is usually kind and generous and keeps diseases away from people. But in some situations Akuj uses illness and disaster to punish someone who commits a serious offense or goes against a vital ritual of the people. Hence Akuj's help is always sought by individual or group prayers said according to need, or by community prayers offered during ceremonies (like weddings) and festive occa-

PROVERBS OF THE TURKANA

Toem apokon, sodi kitoemeta moi iyong ngide kon.

Honor your father, and your children will honor you.

Angatun aite apei ejok edwangit abongun kogin.

Gaining one cow on a cattle raid is better than gaining none.

Akisirmokin aemong kitatae elope erai akingo naapolon.

Never interrupt a man who is giving praise to his favorite bull.
(The favorite bull is the focus of the herd and the center of the family's livelihood. For this reason it is worthy of praise.)

Aelo a ngiputiro ejok noi kotere elose alogita.

Since warthogs go in packs, they must maintain very close friendships.

Akikwaan a akimuj echom ka naitwaan ilereunit atamar arai ngesi ekisikwanet itwaan.

Baboons eat nuts and berries with their fingers as people do, so they must be related to us.

Nyesakene emorotot auno kotere eni elope bon itwaan totwan ori kiridak.

A python doesn't need rope to tie a person up.

Achwaanut a ekolia anakipi ikoni achwaanut aitwaan eyei nawi keng.

A man in his homestead is like a fish in water.

sions. The Turkana believe that when people die they go to Akuj.

Akuj can be approached or appealed to through a special diviner (*imuron Akuj*), who is Akuj's representative on earth among the people. The *imuron Akuj* starts his service to the people by going through a period of preparation that may last variously from a few days to several months. The *imuron Akuj* withdraws alone to a lonely, sacred place where nobody knows what is happening to him and how he is managing to survive. When he returns, the *imuron Akuj* says he can now tell the future through dreams. And as time goes on, he proceeds to heal the sick, to deal with witches and sorcerers, to restore people's fertility, to help make the rain fall. In former times, it was such people who became leaders of raids and battles.

The community is also served by less important diviners (*imuron ekitoit*). These priests act as traditional doctors, fortune-tellers, and ritual cleansers. Witchcraft and curses are believed to have a powerful effect on people's lives. If someone becomes the object of a curse, he or she must seek a diviner's help to break the spell. The Turkana also believe in nature spirits who inhabit mountains, rivers, lakes, and other localities. But they are not thought to have the power to cause evil, and so they are not feared.▲

chapter

6

COLONIALISM AND CONTEMPORARY TURKANA

IN 1895, THE BRITISH DECLARED THE EAST
African Protectorate over what was afterward
renamed the Colony and Protectorate of Kenya.
Three years later, the British led their first mili-
tary expedition into Turkana territory. The
British and the Turkana fought each other several times during that expedition, and relations
between the two remained hostile thereafter.

Following the expedition, the British largely
ignored the Turkana, especially those in the
northern parts, for several years. During that
period, Ethiopia, a large kingdom to the northeast of Turkanaland, began to extend control
over northern Turkana territory. Ethiopians gave
the Turkana guns. They chose respected Turkana
leaders to report to them on their condition, on
disputes with neighbors, and other matters.

Meanwhile, the southern Turkana saw more

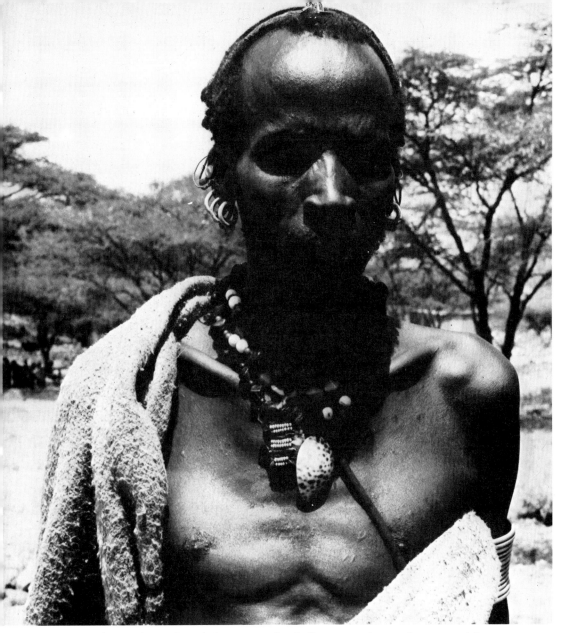

The Turkana faced domination both from people in Ethiopia and from British colonists.

of the British than their northern kinsfolk. They were therefore growing more accustomed to the British presence. Some even paid the taxes that the British demanded, hoping that the British would protect them from cattle-raiding neighbors.

Indeed, the Karamajong Cluster and their neighbors had raided each other's cattle in the past, but by 1910 the situation had begun to change. The introduction of firearms by the British and the Ethiopians made cattle-raiding more dangerous. Also, British colonialists had begun establishing ranches in the fertile parts of central Kenya, and found themselves caught in the middle of these disputes. They wrongly blamed the Turkana for most of the raids, probably because the Turkana attacked in a more organized and flamboyant way than their neighbors. The British decided that for regional peace and security, and for the prosperity of their ranches, the cattle-raiding had to stop.

Under British rule, a few Turkana took up wage jobs in the new center at Kitale, a city to the south of Turkanaland, building rails and roads, while others worked as herdsmen for the European ranchers in parts of Kenya. However, most Turkana remained in their homeland, where two administrative centers were established at Lodwar and Lokitaung, with administrative officers, the Kenya police, local courts, dispensaries, and schools.

To administer the Turkana, the British wanted single Turkana leaders to look after fairly large areas and populations. In the course of time, the British appointed headmen and subheadmen over territorial sections to collect taxes and pass on information about grazing areas. But the

British found that the appointees did not represent the different parts of the territorial sections, and that the Turkana of the mountain areas were not under any headmen and did not pay taxes. Nor did the British find it easy to recruit Turkana as local policemen. The Turkana retained much of their traditional lifestyle, refusing to cooperate with the British.

On their part, the British were not overly zealous about Turkana development. And in spite of the peacekeeping and administrative structures, as well as the missionary schools and medical facilities, in many ways the Turkana remained greatly isolated from developments in the rest of Kenya.

A major drought hit Turkanaland in 1961–62. International agencies set up famine relief camps. The most distressed Turkana settled there until they could get back on their feet after the rains returned. Camps like these still exist to help such people in times of low rain.

In December 1963, Kenya resumed independence. In addition to the camps, the Kenyan government made efforts to improve Turkana living conditions by seeking alternatives to cattle-herding as the primary Turkana livelihood.

In 1965, the Turkana Fishermen's Cooperative Union was formed. The members live largely on fish and also profit from the sale of dried fish. The families who take part tend to earn a good living. By 1987, membership in the

The lives of many Turkana were changed from pastoral to agricultural.

union had reached 5,000. Today, however, there is concern that, if the union grows any more, it will deplete the supply of fish in Lake Turkana.

In 1968, the Kenyan government started irrigated agricultural fields at Kikarongole. Several others have been set up since. They require a great deal of money to keep running and have had only limited success. One major problem is that the rivers that provide the water for irrigation dry up for months a time, bringing the farming to a halt. In recent years, rainwater harvesting technology has been introduced. With it, rain that does not happen to fall on the crops is captured and channeled to them.

Modern education has also recently made

substantial progress among the Turkana. Elementary education is universal and free, though not compulsory, in Kenya. For years the Kenyan government found it very difficult to get Turkana children into school. Turkana children and youths traditionally learn what they need to know by watching and listening to grown-ups, by belonging to age-sets, by initiation and bond-friendships, and by participating in other indigenous practices. And the pastoral Turkana move around so constantly that a full modern school term would be impossible for most children and youths.

Because of the contagious diseases that wiped out large numbers of Turkana cattle in 1979, most children were too poor or ill to attend school. The Kenyan government responded by providing free milk and lunches to students across the country. The government, as well as the missionaries, also built more schools. The government continues to encourage modern education in Turkanaland.

These relief, agricultural, educational, and other development programs have had a considerable effect on the Turkana lifestyle. In four years, the number of Turkana children in elementary school increased from 5,500 to 20,000. Today, almost half the Turkana are settled, no longer completely dependent on pastoralism.

Still, many children in Turkana schools drop out after a few years for a number of reasons.

Songs of the Turkana

The Turkana sing about their daily life. Singing and dancing serve as entertainment during the often uneventful hours of cattle-herding and seasonal migration. They also help keep spirits up in their desert environment, which can make their lifestyle very difficult.

A Woman Casts a Spell

Aberu kimoria ekosim
   kakopito
atotubok nyakamurania

atotub nyelute, nyelute

A woman put a ram's tail into
   some fish,
And fed it to her husband's
   mother.
We must slaughter an animal
   to break the spell.

Cocky Cattle Raiders

Kirama akimi kiwokor
naparan ekiriamia
sua lu ngirujara napis

kimina sua emoit
iyara napis
kimina eya ngatuk
   emoit
kimina sua emoit
iyara napis

We shot and gave chase
On a daytime raid.
They're taking us to the
   police.
We don't care that the enemy
Is taking us to the police.
We had fun raiding Pokot
   cattle.
We don't care that the enemy
Is taking us to the police.

Black Bull

Iriono, iriono todoyo

longurua nyakauwa
iriono ajoketa ngimoyo

nyakauwa, kiseme
   lokadopo

He is dark, dark from head to
   tail,
His back is black.
He is dark and his hooves are
   sound,
He is black with a pretty white
   patch.

The Turkana face the challenge of combining traditional and modern culture.

For one, the children feel that only a few years of education are needed for them to get a job. For another, parents fear that if a daughter receives too much modern education, she will lack the traditional skills that a good Turkana wife needs, in which case her family may not receive a very large bridewealth when she marries.

This parental fear is a good illustration of the conflicts faced today by the Turkana. It is not easy for a traditional culture to assimilate the demands of the modern world. The Turkana have found themselves deeply involved in the debate over their customary pastoral way of life. The Turkana, like the Kenyan government and well-meaning foreigners, wrestle over the questions: What is the best future for the Turkana? Is the pastoral life the best choice, as it has always been? Or do farming and town life offer brighter hopes? Will some combination of old and new methods be best? These are questions that the Turkana will answer as they face the future.▲

Glossary

adakar Neighborhood.

agiboro Wet season.

akotar Marriage ceremony.

Akuj God in Turkana traditional religion.

akumo Dry season.

ateger Clan.

awi Homestead.

ekitela Territory.

Karamajong Cluster Seven related peoples who all speak dialects of the same language, Teso: Turkana, Karamajong, Jie, Dodos, Toposa, Donyiro, Jiye.

Ngabotok Small section of the Turkana who live by farming and honey-gathering.

Ngicuro and Ngimonia "People of the Plains" and "People of the Forest," the two Turkana territories.

Nilotes Peoples whose languages originated near the headwaters of the Nile river.

Pokot Also called Suk; a people living to the southwest of the Turkana.

Samburu A people living to the southeast of the Turkana.

Stones and Leopards The two groups of Turkana initiated men.

talupainon Bond-friendship.

For Further Reading

Berg-Schlosser, Dirk. *Tradition and Change in Kenya*. Munich: Ferdinand Schoning, 1984.

Best, Gunter. *Culture and Language of the Turkana, NW Kenya*. Heidelberg: C. Winter Universitätsverlag, 1983.

Fedders, A. *Turkana Pastoral Craftsmen*. Nairobi: Transafrica, 1977.

Fedders, Andre, and Salvatori, Cynthia. *Peoples and Cultures of Kenya*. Nairobi: TransAfrica, 1979.

Oliver, Roland. *The African Experience*. New York: HarperCollins, 1991.

Challenging Reading
Barrett, Anthony. *Akiyar a ngiturkana/Turkana Way of Life*. Nairobi: 1988.

Dimmendaal, Gerrit Jan. *The Turkana Language*. Dordrecht, The Netherlands; Cinnaminson, NJ: Foris Publications, 1983.

Index

63

ABOUT THE AUTHOR

Professor Chieka Ifemesia holds a professorship in history at the University of Nigeria, Nsukka. He has served as president of Anambra State College of Education Awka. He has taught history at the University of Birmingham in Britain and at the University of California at Los Angeles. He is currently teaching at colleges of the City University of New York.

Professor Ifemesia has published more than thirty articles and four books on African civilization and history.

PHOTO CREDITS: CFM, Nairobi
DESIGN: Kim Sonsky